The Great Frontier

FREEDOM AND HIERARCHY
IN MODERN TIMES

The essays in this volume were delivered as the fourth
CHARLES EDMONDSON HISTORICAL LECTURES
at Baylor University in the spring of 1982.
The Edmondson Lectures are made possible by an
endowment established by Dr. E. Bud Edmondson
of Longview, Texas, to honor his father,
Mr. Charles S. B. Edmondson.

The Great Frontier

FREEDOM AND HIERARCHY
IN MODERN TIMES

William H. McNeill

PRINCETON UNIVERSITY PRESS

PRINCETON, NEW JERSEY

Library of Congress Cataloging in Publication Data will
be found on the last printed page of this book

ISBN 0-691-04658-1

This book has been composed in Linotron Galliard type

Clothbound editions of Princeton University Press books
are printed on acid-free paper, and binding materials are chosen
for strength and durability. Paperbacks, although satisfactory
for personal collections, are not usually suitable
for library rebinding.

Printed in the United States of America by Princeton
University Press, Princeton, New Jersey

Acknowledgments

THESE ESSAYS were originally prepared for delivery at Baylor University, March 31–April 1, 1982, as the fourth Charles Edmondson Historical Lectures. Professor Rufus B. Spain arranged the invitation and chose the topic from among several I suggested; thus he can justly claim part credit for what follows.

Since that time, my colleagues at the University of Chicago—John Coatsworth, David Galenson, Friedrich Katz, and Arthur Mann—improved the text by making suggestions and correcting mistakes in my first formulation. Members of my class in "Human Ecology since 1750," Autumn 1982, also read the manuscript and drew my attention to a few passages needing emendation. Finally, my wife and daughter combed out snarls in my prose with the patient diligence their forebears on the frontier reserved for untangling wool.

For this help, and for the sympathetic enthusiasm of Edward Tenner of Princeton University Press, I am truly grateful.

Chicago   William H. McNeill
January 1983

The Great Frontier

FREEDOM AND HIERARCHY
IN MODERN TIMES

LECTURE I: TO 1750

IN THE LATTER part of the nineteenth century, east coast city dwellers in the United States had difficulty repressing a sense of their own persistent cultural inferiority vis-à-vis London and Paris. At the same time a great many old-stock Americans were dismayed by the stream of immigrants coming to these shores whose diversity called the future cohesion of the Republic into question almost as seriously as the issue of slavery had done in the decades before the Civil War. In such a climate of opinion, the unabashed provinciality of Frederick Jackson Turner's (1861-1932) paper "The Significance of the Frontier in American History," delivered at a meeting of the newly founded American Historical Association in connection with the World Columbian Exposition in Chicago (1892), began within less than a decade to resound like a trumpet call, though whether it signalled advance or retreat remained profoundly ambiguous.

On the one hand, if Turner were to be believed, effete easterners need not have worried about lagging behind European civilization. Instead, a new nation, with a sturdy character of its own, had already formed under western skies, since "the advance of the frontier has meant a steady movement away from the influence of Europe, a steady growth of independence along American lines."[1] National unity and national identity were safe and sound too, because "In the crucible of the frontier the immigrants were Americanized, liberated and fused into a mixed race, English neither in nationality nor characteristics."[2] Persistent cultural difference from Europe was therefore evidence not of inferiority, but of a unique and indigenous response to free land and other freedoms of the

[3]

frontier, since it is "to the frontier that the American intellect owes its striking characteristics."[3]

On the other hand, as Turner was careful to remark in both his first and last sentences, the Bureau of the Census had officially declared the frontier extinct in 1890. What did that portend for the future of American civilization? Might not the frontier-generated uniqueness of the United States decay as rapidly as it had arisen? In Turner's own words: "He would be a rash prophet who should assert that the expansive character of American life has now entirely ceased. . . . But never again will such gifts of free land offer themselves."[4]

The frontier thesis therefore appealed to optimists and pessimists, westerners and easterners alike. The extraordinary attention Turner's idea continues to receive attests the breadth of its resonance within our society.[5]

Some two generations later, Walter Webb (1888-1963) extended Turner's thesis beyond American borders by propounding the idea of a Great Frontier extending all the way around the globe.[6] Webb argued that this Great Frontier had the effect of bringing windfall profits into the European metropolis, and these profits in turn sustained a prolonged era of economic expansion from 1500 onward. Windfalls came in the form of free land for European settlers in Asia, Africa, and Australia as well as in North and South America, and also as a vast treasure trove of easily exploited gold and silver. But after about 1900 frontier windfalls became a thing of the past. The depression of the 1930s, in the midst of which Webb conceived his book, therefore registered the end of the frontier-based era of easy times not just in American but also in world history. In Webb's hands the frontier thesis thus became unambiguously pessimistic as to the future. Partly for that reason, perhaps, his idea has been far less influential than

Turner's, and, except in Texas,[7] was soon rejected by historians and forgotten by the public.

There were compelling reasons for this rejection. World War II and the thirty-year boom that followed certainly seemed to invalidate Webb's gloomy economic prophecies. In addition, after World War II American historians decided that the expansion of Europe was no longer a respectable field of academic endeavor. Instead, it became fashionable to assist the peoples of Asia and Africa in throwing off European imperialism by writing their histories for them.[8] Accordingly, Webb's synoptic vision met short shrift. Experts found that frontiers in Australia, South Africa, and Latin America were not the same as the frontier in North America, where the behavior of French and English pioneers also differed. Meanwhile, Europe itself faded from historians' purview. National, regional, and thematically specialized research took pride of place as professors of European history at American colleges and universities responded to the breakup of European world power and to cheaper transatlantic air fares by trying to rival European scholars at their own game of improving accuracy by exhausting the archives.

There was, however, an oddly isolated intellectual countercurrent in the postwar American academic scene. It stemmed from an effort, funded and sponsored by the Social Science Research Council, to transcend the traditional fragmentation of social studies as embodied in university departments by bringing the entire spectrum of humanistic and social science sensibilities to bear upon the study of a particular human society or some geographical region. Cross disciplinary area studies therefore nurtured large views without ever quite achieving academic respectability.

This was the situation that stimulated Louis Hartz to draw on his American studies background at Harvard to write a provocative book titled *Founding of New Societies: Studies in the History of the United States, Latin America, South Africa, Canada, and Australia* (New York, 1969). Hartz and his associates (for he farmed out detailed analysis of Latin America, South Africa, Canada, and Australia to like-thinking colleagues) found a meaningful pattern in the very diversity of frontier experiences. The local differences that, according to others, discredited Webb's synthetic idea made sense to Hartz because he saw in each overseas transplant a mere fragment of the original complexity of European class structures. Each such segment, torn from its original context, having rooted itself on new ground, subsequently evolved according to a logical dynamic of its own, and departed from the European norm and from other patterns of frontier development because of the fragmentary, lopsided character of the initial transfers.

Such a view affirmed the central importance of the European heritage in determining subsequent social and cultural development. Simultaneously, it emphasized deficiencies in what had been transferred to new ground. Hartz's vision of American culture and society therefore implied, without explicitly affirming, an enduring inferiority of the American "fragment" when compared to the full complexity of the European matrix whence it had been excised. In so characterizing American life he gave fresh voice to cultivated easterners' longstanding alienation from the crudity of the backwoods that Turner and Webb had deemed worthy of celebration. Terms of debate altered: witness the quasi-Marxist epithets "feudal," "bourgeois," and "radical" that Hartz used to characterize his new societies. But the debate continued to pit the effete east against the brash west as before.

Hartz's portrait of frontier societies seems to me therefore quite as provincial as Turner's and just as much in need of refurbishing. And refurbish we must if the history of the United

[6]

States, taken as a whole, is to become really intelligible once again. For if we want to make sense of all the local, ethnic, and thematic dimensions of the American past, to which professional historians have devoted their principal efforts of late, we very much need a framework into which the entire national experience in all its facets will somehow fit. Otherwise more and more facts, however well attested in the sources, become a burden on the memory, and the study of our history runs the risk of turning into mere antiquarianism.

The trouble is that the over-optimistic view of earlier generations who saw the meaning of American history in material progress, guaranteed and sustained by liberty as experienced on the frontier and codified into the Constitution, now seems inadequate. Too many people were left out: blacks, women, ethnics.

Class consciousness, even in Louis Hartz's modulated form, turned out to be an entirely inadequate substitute. This was not solely because, as the official ideology of an unfriendly power, Marxism carried a taint of treason in post-World War II United States. The real deficiency of Marxist views was that class differences did not accurately coincide with the rather more acute ethnic, religious, and racial fissures in American society. Moreover, a vision emphasizing class struggle disrupted nationwide unity and fellow feeling and exacerbated frictions with other human beings who were uncomfortably close at hand. Accordingly, Marxist versions of United States history have remained sectarian, quite incapable of remedying the inadequacies of the older, evangelical and liberal, vision of our past.

Professional response among historians was to concentrate on detail, hoping that from more and more facts a better portrait of the whole would somehow emerge, quite of its own accord. But histories of all the various groupings into which

Americans have consciously divided themselves, and might be divided by historians in retrospect, do not add up to a history of the nation as a whole any more than separate histories of each county in each state, if set side by side on library shelves, would provide a substitute for a history of the United States. Fragmented vision and close attention to detail do not necessarily improve accuracy. Focusing on separate trees may obscure the forest; preoccupation with an infinitude of differing leaves may allow the tree itself to disappear from view. Every increase in historical detail, in other words, risks losing sight of larger patterns which may be more important for public action and understanding than anything segmented sub-histories can discover.

The opposite extreme of looking at the history of this nation as part of a far larger process of European expansion may seem calculated to deprive the United States of its uniqueness. But if appropriately modulated to recognize both differences and uniformities, it seems to me that this perspective provides a far more adequate and comprehensive vision of our past than anything older nationalistic histories of liberty and prosperity had to offer. It puts the United States back into the world as one of a family of peoples and nations similarly situated with respect to the old centers of European civilization. Moreover, by taking seriously the Great Frontier phenomenon of modern times, we will find plenty of room for the downtrodden and poor as well as for the rich and successful, and thus avoid one of the main reproaches leveled against the liberal, establishmentarian version of the American past.

Here lay Webb's great achievement. He offered an appropriate framework for reappraising the history of this country by recognizing that our past was part of a global process of civilizational expansion. Progress and liberty, so dear to our forebears, played a part in the process; but so did their op-posites—slavery and the destruction of all those non-European cultures and societies that got in the way. By accepting such a framework, therefore, the successes *and* the failures can all find appropriate scope in our history if we are wise and sensitive enough to see the persistent double-edgedness of change—destroying *and* preserving, denying *and* affirming established values of human life, everywhere and all the time.

Foolhardy though it may be, this is what I propose to undertake in these lectures. Foolhardy—but not impossible: for what matters is perspective and proportion, not detail.

· · ·

WEBB'S Great Frontier, like Turner's, was a region where men with skills derived from Europe met Amerindians and other "savage" peoples who were quite unable to resist the advances of white settlers. The "free land" that white men appropriated was land once used by others. The expansion of one society occurred only at the cost of another's destruction. As such, the American frontier was merely an extreme case of contact and collision between societies at different levels of skill—a pattern that runs throughout recorded history, and constitutes one of the main themes of the human past.

When peoples of approximately equal levels of skill, numbers, and organization meet on a frontier, drastic geographical displacements are unlikely. Minor fluctuations in the demarcation zone can be expected, with fluctuations in the incidence of victory and defeat. But as long as the parties remain nearly equal, no very drastic change can, by definition, occur. Minor borrowing back and forth is to be expected. Techniques and ideas that for some reason have novelty value may pass from one society to its neighbor. But it is only when inherited institutions on one side of the demarcation line cease to work well that more fundamental change becomes in the least likely, for most human beings most of the time prefer the safe and familiar to anything new. When, however, institutional decay weakens effective resistance to alien pressure, world-historical changes may ensue. Civilizational benchmarks like those signalized by Alexander's conquests of western Asia and Egypt, the Germanic invasions of the Roman empire, or the Moslem conquests of the Middle East and northern Africa record these extraordinary shifts.

Such events are rare and exceptional inasmuch as they fall outside the range of everyday encounters. An ordinary and therefore more important frontier phenomenon arose whenever one society abutted upon another that was somewhat less or more skilled. When the skill-short participant in such an encounter became aware of the difference, efforts to borrow skills needed to catch up and overtake the stronger neighbor were likely to follow. Alternatively, the weaker party might undertake measures to strengthen home defenses against an alien way of life that seemed to threaten something precious in the local cultural heritage. Far-ranging, deep-going social transformations may be triggered by either reaction.

This, indeed, seems to me to be the principal drive wheel of historic change. Encounters with strangers whose ways were different, and often threatening as well, were in all probability the main factor provoking and propagating inventions from the most ancient times to the present. And from the time when crossroads societies first achieved skills distinctly superior to those of their neighbors, i.e., since civilization first appeared on this earth, incessant interaction between more skilled and less skilled peoples has been in train. The upshot, despite numerous back-eddies and local breakdowns of civilized complexity, has been an ineluctable expansion of the portions of the globe subjected to or incorporated within civilized social structures.

Inside any given civilization an analogous interaction may

also be detected between center and periphery, capital and provinces, upper and lower classes. For civilized societies were created and are sustained by dint of occupational differentiation and specialization. Varying skills and conflicting interests therefore divide civilized communities against themselves. Such internal frictions and differentiation merge with the polarity between civilized and fringe "barbarian" communities by almost imperceptible degrees, for civilizational boundaries are always imprecise.

My proposition boils down to the assertion that cultural differentiation generated historical change, whether within a civilized society, or across its borders. Climatic and other limits of course checked the interactive process. Agricultural skills could not readily be transferred to desert land. Disease barriers were also often important in checking expansion of dense forms of human settlement onto new ground. Protection costs against hostile military harassment were sometimes too high for cultivators to sustain on ground otherwise propitious for them. For all these reasons, the cultural landscape of the earth never approached uniformity, even though the high skills initially confined to a few civilized centers did tend to spread to new places as the generations succeeded one another.[9]

As long as patterns of transport and communication changed slowly, cultural interaction proceeded century after century without generating a frontier of the sort Turner and Webb celebrated. Differences between adjacent peoples were kept within relatively modest bounds because new skills diffused in short bursts across limited distances and among peoples of nearly equivalent levels of knowledge and organization. A few conspicuous gaps, like that between steppe nomads and settled agriculturalists, became chronic, based, as they were, on contrasting human adaptations to enduring geographical diversity.

The gap between pastoral and agricultural societies long remained critically important in the Old World. This was because important zones where nomads penetrated tilled land existed across a broad region of the eastern hemisphere: along the edges of the African savanna, and across the borders of the even more extensive steppe and desert lands of Eurasia. From the time when pastoral nomads first learned to shoot arrows from horseback, about 800 B.C., until the fourteenth century A.D., military advantage consistently rested with the peoples of the desert and steppe who moved faster, and could therefore concentrate superior force at a given locality almost at will. The political history of civilized Eurasia and of Africa, in fact, consists largely of intermittent conquest by invaders from the grasslands, punctuated by recurrent rebellions of agricultural populations against subjugation to the heirs of such conquerors. Only at the two extremes of the Old World, in Japan and western Europe, were these rhythms of alternating nomad conquest and agricultural revolt too weak to matter very much.[10]

So far as I can tell, an "open" frontier of the kind that developed in North and South America, Australia, and South Africa after 1500 never arose in earlier times. Perhaps when neolithic farming folk first spread their fields across Eurasia, penetrating forests where hunting bands had previously roamed, something faintly analogous to the modern frontier arose. But that happened long before the dawn of recorded history, and the archaeological record does not show whether the advance of agriculture involved wholesale displacement of populations, as on the American frontier, or whether hunters already on the ground simply learned from neighbors how to supplement their kill by making fields and raising crops. Both processes presumably were at work, in what proportion no one can tell.

The closest analogue to the modern frontier phenomenon

in the deeper past seems to be the expansion of Chinese society southward from its original home in the Yellow River valley. Chinese colonization started before 800 B.C., and continued sporadically to the present. It was therefore a relatively slow, massive, and sustained process, involving the wholesale remodelling of natural landscapes. The Chinese built rice paddies as they advanced, leveling each field precisely, and arranging for suitable inflow of water so as to keep the surface submerged during the growing season. On most larger streams, effective water management required canal construction, diking, and other improvements to natural water courses. The settlers thereby created a transport network that tied China's expanding body politic together as effectively—perhaps, indeed, more effectively—than did the Confucian bureaucracy that oversaw the whole effort.

Like the ponderous, slow-moving Pleistocene ice sheets, whose scouring action transformed the landscape of northern Eurasia and much of North America, the expanding human mass of Chinese settlers engulfed earlier inhabitants of the Yangtze valley and regions farther south, incorporating them into the Chinese world. Human numbers and the enormous investment of labor, skill, and organization involved in making the natural landscape over into paddy fields surrounded and then submerged earlier occupants. Military action played very little part in the process. What mattered were the picks, shovels, and hoes of countless millions of pioneers, laboring persistently year after year after year, under the direction of government officials.[11]

Perhaps Andean civilization expanded in pre-Columbian times in a similar fashion. Certainly the abandoned terraces that still cling to Peruvian mountainsides constitute an impressive monument to past human effort. The taming of other regions to agriculture must also have involved prolonged, anonymous

[13]

human labor on a massive scale. But until modern times, nowhere, so far as I know, did the process involve ingestion of one population by another on anything approaching the scale that occurred across the Chinese southern frontier. That was because the Chinese had skills as farmers and water engineers that contiguous peoples lacked, and were ready to submit to a labor discipline that others resisted. China's historic magnitude, cohesion, and population density resulted—traits quite unparalleled elsewhere.[12]

But China's slow-moving frontier paled before the extraordinary circumstances that confronted Europeans after 1500. For the overseas expansion that followed hard on the heels of European voyages of discovery was matched by a landward expansion of almost comparable significance. European settlers began to drift into the Ukraine and adjacent areas of the western steppe in the sixteenth century, finding empty or almost empty grasslands awaiting them. This was because older nomad populations had shrunk back, retreating in all likelihood from exposure to bubonic plague, which had become endemic among the burrowing rodents of the western steppe in the fourteenth century.[13] In the course of the next two hundred years, the western steppe was firmly incorporated into European agricultural society by Slavic and Rumanian pioneers who did the work, acting, for the most part, under the legal control of noble estate owners and entrepreneurs, often of a different nationality.

The scope of this "eastward movement" bears comparison with the more familiar westward movement across North America. Expansion of agriculture into the drier and more easterly portions of the steppe continued sporadically throughout the nineteenth and into the twentieth centuries. The latest episode came in the 1950s, when the Russians plowed up millions of acres of marginal steppe lands in Kazakhstan in order to remedy the persistent grain shortages that had long plagued their planning.

Europe's landward frontier extended northward through forested land as well. There, agriculture was seldom practicable but fur-bearing animals abounded. Medieval fur traders, operating from such northern cities as Novgorod, successfully solved the problems of long-distance travel and survival in the Arctic and sub-Arctic regions of northern Russia. Once across the Urals (by 1580), therefore, Russian fur traders could move from one Siberian river system to another by making a series of easy portages. This they already knew how to do. Consequently, explorers reached Okhotsk on the Pacific coast as early as 1637. A vast land, thinly populated by weakly organized hunters and gatherers, thus came under Russian control. A little later, but in almost the same fashion, other fur traders, operating from Montreal (after 1642) and from the shores of Hudson Bay (after 1670) extended their control over the Canadian Arctic. As is well known, the rival fur-trading empires met in the 1780s when Russian pioneers who had crossed to Alaska collided with British, American, and Spanish claimants to the Pacific coastlands of North America.[14]

Because of our national origins, we in this country are far more conscious of the overseas dimension of Europe's expansion. Nor is this merely the result of myopic local perspective. European ships did in fact inaugurate more drastic new encounters after 1500 than anything happening overland within Eurasia. This justifies us in giving pride of place to European frontiers overseas, for nothing in earlier ages can quite compare with the revolution in older human balances inaugurated by those famous voyages—Columbus to Magellan, 1492-1521—so remarkably concentrated into a single generation.

Thereafter, Europeans commanding skills accumulated across millennia of civilized history found themselves face to face previously isolated and therefore low-skilled peoples in many parts of the earth. In Australia, for example, to cite the most extreme case, European intruders met aborigines whose way of life, as attested archaeologically, seems to have altered very little after their initial penetration of the continent thousands of years before. Even in the New World, where far more accomplished Amerindian societies, like those of Mexico and Peru, came up against Spanish conquistadors, they, too, proved quite unable to resist the newcomers. Numbers were all on the side of the Amerindians at first. Spanish skills and organization, though undoubtedly superior, were not so enormously above the levels attained by the Aztecs and Incas as to compensate for the small numbers of those who followed Cortez and Pizarro, whether at the time of their conquests, or subsequently. But European epidemiological superiority was indubitable and decisive. Inherited and acquired immunities to a formidable array of lethal infections allowed Europeans to survive in the presence of killers such as smallpox, measles, flu, tuberculosis, diphtheria, and others, whereas the inexperienced Amerindians proved vulnerable to wholesale destruction on first encountering these infections.[15]

Lethal diseases from Europe and, ere long, also from Africa (yellow fever and malaria in particular) demoralized survivors and paralyzed Amerindian efforts to mount resistance against European political and cultural domination. In many places, depopulation became almost total, leaving unoccupied land for European settlers to appropriate freely. Thus the "empty" frontier Turner spoke of arose from the destruction of Amerindian populations by infections imported from the Old World, sporadically reinforced by resort to armed force. Similar epidemiological disasters afflicted other formerly isolated inhabitants of Oceania, South Africa, and, indeed, wherever a disease-inexperienced population encountered disease-resistant pioneers and explorers. Siberian hunters and trappers met the same fate when Russian fur traders initiated contacts with them, for example; and Eskimos in the Canadian Arctic were experiencing a parallel catastrophe as recently as the 1940s.[16]

The combination of epidemiological superiority with a greater or lesser superiority of skills on the part of intrusive Europeans was what gave the Great Frontier its unique character.

Nevertheless, it is worth emphasizing that not all the uncivilized parts of the earth were hospitable to European penetration. Until about 1850, tropical Africa was very effectively guarded by a formidable array of local diseases which mowed down European and Asian intruders as ruthlessly as European diseases mowed down previously isolated people of the temperate zones. African peoples of the rain forest and savanna south of the Sahara therefore remained in undisturbed possession of their ancestral lands. The slave trade soon assumed hitherto unexampled scale among them, supplying labor to European-managed plantations in the New World and to Moslem households and plantations in the Old in approximately equal numbers.[17] Slave raiding undoubtedly altered older patterns of human life in Africa in far-reaching ways. Simultaneously, the spread of maize and of other new crops from America began to provide a far more productive basis for African agriculture. Changes must have been drastic under these circumstances. But Africa did *not* become a theater for European frontier expansion save for a small area in the extreme south, where a cooler, drier climate prevented tropical diseases from spreading.

Before 1750, therefore, the steppe and forest zones of Eurasia, together with North and South America, constituted the principal regions where frontier encounters assumed the extraordinary form familiar to us from our own national history. This was where Europeans could and did begin to occupy

[17]

land emptied, or almost emptied, of older inhabitants by the catastrophic juxtaposition of disease-experienced civilized populations with epidemiologically and culturally[18] vulnerable natives. Nothing comparable had ever happened before. European expansion therefore assumed unparalleled proportions. The process gave birth to the two politically dominant states of our own time, the USSR and the USA, one east and the other west of the older centers of European civilization. Brazil and the diverse states of Spanish America are likewise heirs of this frontier. So is South Africa; but the European encroachment on Australia, New Zealand, and other Pacific islands did not begin until after the middle of the eighteenth century and so does not yet enter our purview.

The most salient characteristic of the Great Frontier created by the combined ravages of civilized diseases, alcohol, and firearms on indigenous populations was that human numbers were or soon became scant in the contact zone. Anyone who wished to exploit the land agriculturally or sought to mine precious metals or extract other raw materials faced a problem of finding an adequate labor force to do the necessary work. Shortage of manpower meant that European skills and knowledge could not readily be brought to bear in frontier lands, no matter how richly they were endowed.

Carrying Europeans across the seas to remedy this situation was expensive. Relatively few ever made the crossing before the 1840s, when steamships began to cheapen passage and to enlarge passenger carrying capacity. Estimates of transatlantic migration are very inexact, since early records of voyages across the ocean are spotty at best and seldom include passenger lists. A recent guess set the total of British immigrants to North America before 1780 at 750,000 and of French to Canada at only 10,000.[19] Further south no careful calculation of any general total of European immigration exists, though what scraps of evidence there are suggest that something like a million persons crossed the ocean to take up residence in the Caribbean and Latin America before 1800.[20]

Spaniards did, of course, employ Amerindians in the mines and for innumerable building projects and other enterprises in the first rush of their conquest. But the extreme vulnerability of such a labor force to epidemic disease led to heavy loss of life and soon made recruitment difficult. In most islands of the Caribbean the Amerindian population died out completely. Amerindians also disappeared almost totally from the coastal regions of the Caribbean, where African diseases reinforced the destructive power of those imported from Europe. Enslaved Africans, however, could and soon did provide a more disease-resistant labor force for plantation agriculture and other economic enterprises in the New World. Relatively precise calculation of the number of slaves carried from Africa is possible because the traffic came to be conducted by specialized slave ships, whose number and carrying capacity can be established with some accuracy. A recent estimate puts the number of Africans brought to the New World before 1820 at 7.8 million; and the same authority suggests that this figure is four to five times the contemporaneous total of European migration across the Atlantic.[21]

This perhaps surprising statistic ought to remind us of how important compulsory labor became and long remained in the New World. Compulsion bulks even larger in our perspective when we remember that most of the Europeans who crossed the Atlantic before steamships cheapened the cost of passage came as unfree indentured servants. Between 300,000 and 400,000 such persons left Britain for North America between 1650 and 1780, according to the best available estimates. This figure amounts to something between half and three-quarters of all the whites who came to North America from Europe before the American revolution.[22] Indentured servants could, of course, look forward to becoming free men if they survived the period of their indentured labor. But as long as their bondage lasted—often seven years—their legal position vis-à-vis their master was not much different from that of black slaves, though the absence of physical differentiation in outward appearance may have made it easier for them to run away before completing their contracts.

The free, egalitarian, and neo-barbarian style of frontier life, so dear to Turner and his followers, did of course exist in North America. It arose wherever export trade failed to thrive during the early stages of colonization. But in the more favored and accessible regions, where European skills proved capable of producing marketable wealth on a relatively large scale, frontier conditions ordinarily provoked not freedom but a social hierarchy steeper than anything familiar in Europe itself. The reason was that commercially precocious frontier societies usually found it necessary to assure the availability and subordination of a labor force by imposing stern legal restrictions on freedom to choose and change occupation. Hence, slave plantations and gangs of indentured servants in the Americas, as well as the serf-cultivated estates of eastern Europe, were quite as characteristic of the frontier as were the free and independent farmers and jacks-of-all-trades whom we habitually associate with frontier life.

One form of export trade that often played a prominent role on the frontier did impose a close symbiosis of equalitarian freedom with bureaucratic hierarchy. Capturing and collecting existing goods—whether furs, placer gold, raw rubber from the Amazon rain forest, or codfish from the Grand Banks—could only be done by a dispersed work force, operating beyond any manager's control. Trans-oceanic marketing of such goods, on the other hand, required comparatively large-scale organization.[23] Trading companies solved this problem by stationing agents at strategic locations, where they conducted a barter trade with the men who did the actual collecting. Commodities exchanged were sufficiently valuable to the parties concerned to bear the cost of transport; and even at remote locations, agents could still be controlled by their home offices since everyone knew that if they failed to send back adequate amounts of the sought-after commodity, the flow of trade goods needed for barter would promptly dry up.

Though a few big trading companies thus managed to span the forbidding distances between European metropolitan centers and the frontier, it remained the case that frontier conditions could not sustain the elaborately graded hierarchy that prevailed in the heartlands of European civilization. Near the center, long tradition and market constraints combined to fit men and women into an elaborately interlocking and largely hereditary pattern of occupations. Legal differentiation separated clergy, nobles, and commoners, and defined membership in a great variety of privileged corporations. In skilled trades, apprentices were bound to their masters for a period of years under conditions that somewhat resembled indentured labor in America. In all these senses, labor was subject to legal coercion in Europe too. But slavery was unimportant; serfdom had disappeared from the most active centers of European economic life long before Columbus sailed; and the price system, acting through fluctuating wages, was becoming increasingly effective in allocating and reallocating labor among competing occupations. Large-scale undertakings like mining and shipping could recruit the necessary manpower by offering appropriate rates of pay. Even soldiering had become a question of fulfilling a contract freely entered into, at least in principle; though once enlisted, a soldier, more even than an indentured servant or apprentice, faced severe penalties for seeking to withdraw from his place in the ranks.

Western Europe's reliance on the market as a means of allocating and reallocating labor among alternative employments was sustained by birth and survival rates that were high enough to supply hands for existing enterprises with a few left over for promising new ventures as well. Legal compulsion, backed by force, became quite unnecessary when enough labor presented itself spontaneously for carrying out all the tasks that the rulers and managers of society felt were really necessary and important. Under such circumstances, compulsion became a waste of time and effort, and a needless provocation as well.

The balance of supply and demand for labor was always precarious. The Black Death in the fourteenth century set back European population for more than a century and altered wage rates abruptly. Thereafter, recurrent epidemics, concentrated especially in towns, frequently cut back on local populations, sometimes very sharply.[24] But such perturbations were rapidly made good by accelerated influx from the healthier countryside, where all those youths who were unable to count on inheriting rights to enough cultivable land to live as their parents were doing constituted a pool of ready recruits for any venture that promised escape from what was, within the village confines, a radically unsatisfactory career prospect. Europe's remarkable record of expansion at home and abroad, dating back to about A.D. 900, rested on a demographic pattern that regularly provided a surplus of rural youths for export to towns and armies, with a few left over for migration to more distant frontier zones as well.

But Europe's demographic balance, elaborate social hierarchy, and the well-established interdependence of social classes could not be reproduced on the frontier. Local population was inadequate. Large-scale enterprise that required major input of labor could not be carried on without compulsion. This was as true of the overland as of the overseas frontier. The legal enserfment of Russian peasants in the seventeenth century differed only slightly from the slavery of American plantations; and debt peonage imposed on Amerindians in the New World, as well as English indentured labor, had the same practical effect, even if the obligated human beings retained rights under these legal systems that were denied to black slaves.

The whole point was to keep slaves, serfs, indentured servants, and peons at work on tasks a managerial, owning class wanted to see accomplished. In proportion to their success, a flood of new goods—sugar, cotton, silver, wheat, indigo, and many more—entered European and world markets. Income thus accruing to enterprising landowners, mine operators, and resident factors for wholesale merchants based in Europe allowed them to buy expensive imported European products so that they could live like gentlemen—more or less. In this fashion a slender simulacrum of European polite society quickly arose in American and European frontier lands. Subsequently, in proportion as local population grew so that labor became available for various crafts and retail commercial occupations, an approximation to European forms of society could gradually develop in the shadow of the planter-landowner-managerial class.

The prominence of slavery and serfdom in European frontier expansion did not foreclose the egalitarian alternative entirely, even in societies dominated by compulsory labor. Runaways and individuals who had worked out their indenture could and did take off into the backwoods to carve out a life free of any obligation to social superiors. Such pioneers often cut themselves off from any but sporadic contacts with civilization. But, like planters and landowners of the frontier, they

[23]

continued to depend for some critically important items on sources of supply far in the rear. Guns and ammunition, as well as iron for tools, were things that even the most remote frontiersmen found it hard to do without. How they got possession of such goods is often unclear. Hand-to-hand swapping could reach far beyond organized markets; and incentive to swapping was real enough since the frontier could usually be made to yield something precious and portable—furs, placer gold, or the like—that commanded a high enough price on world markets to justify its carriage across many miles of plain and mountain.

Hence even the most remote and barbarous *coureurs de bois* of North America, the *bandierantes* of Brazil, the *gauchos* of the pampas, the *vortrekkers* of South Africa, and the Cossacks of Siberia retained a significant and vitally important link with the nearest outposts of civilization. Like the slave-owners and serf-owners of the frontier they, too, participated in the world market system that centered in western Europe. Their participation shrank in proportion as their mode of life descended toward local self-sufficiency. But complete autarky meant loss of the margin of superiority newcomers enjoyed vis-à-vis older native inhabitants. Those who cut loose entirely from Europe-centered and -managed trade nets simply merged into local indigenous populations, and thereupon ceased to act as agents of frontier expansion. Such persons were always few, since the status of a man without access to a gun (and other European-made goods) diminished drastically in remote communities.

The sharp polarization in frontier society between freedom and hierarchy should therefore be understood as arising from alternative responses to the overriding reality of the frontier, to wit, the drastic shortage of labor. For this reason, one social structure was capable of abrupt transmutation into its opposite. Runaway slaves or serfs who made good an escape

[24]

from their master's control at once became egalitarian frontiersmen. The maroons of Jamaica constituted the most famous such community, but were only one of many. On Europe's other flank, Cossack hordes in their early days recruited runaway serfs as a matter of course; later, after the hordes were themselves captured by the Russian state, such escape became illegal, though successful flight into the depths of Siberia continued to occur as long as Russian serfdom endured.

The opposite transmutation from egalitarianism to legally imposed hierarchy was even more common. In the east, wholesale enserfment of once-free peasant populations was the order of the day when frontier expansion into the steppelands got seriously underway in the seventeenth and eighteenth centuries. In the New World, the rise of peonage in Mexico in the sixteenth and seventeenth centuries was analogous. Efforts to transplant reinvigorated forms of manorial jurisdiction to Canada and New York met with scant success; and indentured labor provided only a precarious basis for gentlemen farmers in Virginia and Maryland in the seventeenth and eighteenth centuries. But such efforts show that the urge to impose legal bonds on free men operated in English, Dutch, and French colonial society as well as on the Russian and Spanish frontiers.

We are accustomed to thinking of the equalitarian alternative as the norm of frontier life. Both Turner and Webb, for example, skip over the role of slavery in the frontier history of the United States. I suppose this remarkable omission arose from the fact that they cherished an ideal of American liberty and equality, and also felt nostalgia for the days of their youth when residues of the Wisconsin and west Texas forms of frontier life still dominated local society. By noticing only one aspect of frontier reality, Turner and Webb were able to combine these sentiments uninhibitedly. But this kind of wishful

[25]

thinking deserves to be subjected to skeptical examination. If one does so, it seems to me that a neutral observer would have to conclude that compulsion and legally reinforced forms of social hierarchy were more generally characteristic of frontier society than were equality and freedom.

Two reasons for this circumstance suggest themselves. First of all, free and equal nuclear families scattered thinly over the landscape are in a poor position to protect themselves. Consequently, wherever safeguard from enemy raiding parties was important, the radical equalitarianism of isolated pioneer homesteads proved inadequate. Even in the American west, the U.S. cavalry was called upon to shield settlers from raiding Indians. In the Old World, exposure to violence was far more serious, since, beginning in the 1480s, the Crimean Tartars organized systematic raids across the Ukrainian steppes to supply the insatiable Ottoman slave market. Scattered householders could not mount effective self-defense against such manhunts. Only specialized military organizations—whether the Cossack hordes or the Tsar's regular army—could confront raiding Tartars on more or less even terms. Consequently, for pioneering cultivators of the soil, the price of security from Tartar raids was subjection to experts in violence who could maintain an effective, professionalized frontier defense. Heartfelt efforts to reaffirm vanishing social equality and freedom within the framework of the Cossack horde were nullified by the fact that the Russian state made the horde itself into a privileged corporation after 1648. By exempting enrolled Cossacks from the obligations of serfdom, the Tsar acquired a new and formidable instrument for defending the frontier and imposing serfdom on the rest of the population of the Ukrainian borderlands. Thereafter, Tartar slave raids quickly ceased to be profitable, and the rich grasslands of the western steppe became safe for agricultural settlement on a massive scale.[25]

Because North America was less exposed to military threat than the Eurasian steppelands, American frontier experience gave more scope to the egalitarian, libertarian alternative than did the Russian. Important divergences in our societies still bear witness to this difference. But it was not the frontier per se that dictated this result. Instead it was our unusually low protection costs during the three centuries from 1608 to 1917. Australia, too, enjoyed negligible protection costs until even more recently than the United States, whereas Boer Vortrekkers encountered quite formidable rivals in the kaffir tribesmen with whom they disputed rights to land and water for nearly two centuries. Australia's populist egalitarianism was therefore free to flourish at the expense of imported hierarchies of class and culture, whereas Boer anarchic and egalitarian traditions were tempered by recurrent acceptance of military subordination to commanders whose authority was as great as it was temporary.

A second factor militating against equality and freedom on the frontier was economic. Dependence on supplies from the rear meant that pioneers were chronically at the mercy of merchants and suppliers who, by controlling transportation, controlled the terms of trade. When frontiersmen needed little, and rarely bought or sold anything, this did not infringe upon their liberty very much. But when buying and selling increased in importance so that everyday life began to depend on it, then the few who controlled access to distant markets were in a very favorable position to enhance their income at the expense of the ordinary farmer, miner or fur trapper.

In other words, land ownership and control over a labor force legally tied to the spot was not always necessary to allow a few to exploit the labor of others. This was the burden of

[27]

populist protest against railroads and other outside capitalist interests that became such a prominent feature of United States politics in the second half of the nineteenth century. The Hudson's Bay Company, John Jacob Astor, and the Stroganov company that dominated the Siberian fur trade were no more popular with the backwoodsmen of an earlier age. London and Lisbon merchants who supplied Virginia planters and Brazilian slave owners had a similar relationship with their aristocratic trade partners, while the grain dealers and shipowners who carried grain from Danzig and Odessa to European markets were also in an advantageous position to dictate terms to Polish and Russian landowners.

In all such situations, traders with connections back to the distant markets and workshops of Europe represented the entering wedge for the social complexity and occupational differentiation that was and remained the special hallmark of civilization. Men who bought cheap and sold dear, and made chaffering over prices into a way of life, were disliked and even hated by frontier dwellers—rich and poor, owners and workers, free and bond. Recurrent pogroms against Jews in eastern Europe attest this fact all too poignantly. But frontiersmen could not get on without such people either. Goods otherwise inaccessible were too attractive and too important to do without, even if the purchaser felt cheated in every deal. The only alternative to importation was local manufacture: and in some Ukrainian towns as well as in American cities artisan trades had begun to take root before 1750. Social complexity grew accordingly. Little by little civilization was encroaching.

Nevertheless, prior to 1750 the replication of cosmopolitan complexity and of a graded hierarchy of social classes in peripheral regions of the European world system remained incomplete and sporadic. Until after that date the European em-

[28]

pires arising from the first two modern centuries of expansion remained in place, and were, in fact, growing with each passing decade. That political fact registered the imperfect diffusion of civilized skills and techniques from center to periphery. After 1776, as the process of civilized expansion continued, political patterns changed, signalizing a more complete transfer of the arts and skills of civilization onto new ground. In addition, a new demographic regime in Europe provided a basis for far more massive emigration than had previously occurred.

My next lecture will consider aspects of this second phase in the history of the Great Frontier.

LECTURE II: FROM 1750

THE FIRST of these lectures argued that frontier conditions distorted the social pyramid of European society either by flattening it drastically toward equality and anarchic freedom or, alternatively, by steepening the gradient so as to divide frontiersmen between owners and managers, on the one hand, and an enslaved, enserfed, or debt-coerced work force, on the other. The frontier in other words was neutral as between freedom and compulsion; but the actual balance tipped toward legally sharpened hierarchy because both the need for protection and the prospect of profit pulled in that direction. Before 1750 the freedom and equality we like to associate with frontier life were marginal. The norm was enslavement since only in that way could thinly populated frontier lands participate actively in the world market, and, if need be, also sustain a costly armed establishment.

The starkness of frontier alternatives began to soften after 1750. Two factors pushed in that direction. First of all, an ever-denser network of communication and transportation connecting the center to the periphery tended to flatten the cultural slopes within the European world system, reducing contrasts between each constituent part. Secondly, a new demographic regime accelerated population growth in most of the civilized world. This tended to diminish the labor shortages that had initially provoked both the anarchic and the authoritarian forms of frontier society.

Let me begin with some remarks about the second of these factors, for it was the onset of a new demographic regime about the middle of the eighteenth century which justifies dividing these lectures at the year 1750.

Demographic historians are far from agreed as to what may explain the onset of systematic population growth in the second half of the eighteenth century. But there is no longer any doubt that a change took place, not only in Europe but also in China and the Americas, and probably in India and Africa as well. Warmer and drier climate brought better harvests to northwestern Europe; but such an alteration in climate must have had diverse consequences for farming in other regions of the earth. In the Middle East, for instance, if it also became warmer and drier (which is not known to be the case), then the effect would be to damage crop yields and favor pastoralism. This may well have happened; evidence is simply not in hand. But since the Middle East does not seem to have shared in the rest of the world's eighteenth-century population increase, the hypothesis of an unfavorable climate change there is surely worth investigating along the lines that have been pioneered in Europe.[1]

Another factor operative throughout the Old World was the spread of American food crops as supplements to older kinds of nourishment. Maize, potatoes, sweet potatoes, peanuts, and tomatoes—to name but the most important—allowed peoples in China, Africa, Europe, and elsewhere to increase local production of food, sometimes very substantially. By interspersing old and new crops, as usually happened, risk of failure was diminished. Sometimes new crops did not displace old ones at all, since they could be grown on previously uncropped ground. In northern Europe, for example, it was possible to substitute potatoes for grain-fallow, thus abruptly increasing total food production. In China, too, sweet potatoes grew well on hilly ground that was unsuited to rice paddies. Even when this sort of pure gain was not feasible, American crops often improved the food supply because they yielded more calories per acre than anything known before. Maize was valued in Africa and southern Europe for this reason. Tomatoes, on the other hand, provided vitamins otherwise lacking, especially in Mediterranean and Indian diets. Almost everywhere, in short, American crops expanded available food supplies, sometimes very greatly. The catch was that the new crops required extra labor. They all had to be hoed and weeded during the growing season whereas wheat and other Old World grains (except rice) did not.

Without American food crops, the population growth that began in the Old World during the eighteenth century probably could not have continued for very long. But in and of itself, the availability of new, labor-intensive crops does not seem sufficient to explain systematic population growth, since, without an expanding supply of manpower, American crops could not have spread as fast and as far as they did.[2]

Historical demographers have therefore looked at changes in marriage age, fertility, and other indices of population dynamics. Meticulous and ingenious work with parish records in France and England has indeed shown some changes, but none seems adequate to account for systematic population increase all round the earth. What does appear from such studies, however, is a decrease in the severity of periodic die-off due to epidemic infection. In some instances improvements in medicine may have made a difference by reducing the ravages of plague and smallpox, but the most powerful explanation as to why epidemics became less destructive is to suppose that as communications nets became denser throughout the civilized world, an intensified circulation of lethal diseases left fewer adults at risk. Obviously, whenever lethal infections became endemic or returned at very frequent intervals, all but newborn infants and small children would already have been exposed. And for many infections, exposure provoked lifelong immunity. Lethality therefore concentrated among the very

[33]

young. Replacement of such infant deaths was relatively easy and cost far less than was the case before the eighteenth century, when more sporadic communications left persons of childbearing years also exposed.[3]

Changes in human numbers resulting from the new demographic regime that set in after 1750 were drastic indeed. China's population doubled from about 150 million in 1700 to 313 million in 1794,[4] while Europe's population rose from about 118 million in 1700 to about 187 million in 1801. Within Europe, the most rapid growth came on the two flanks. In Great Britain, population swelled from about 5.8 million in 1700 to 9.15 million in 1801, while Russia's population increased from about 12.5 million in 1724 to some 21 million in 1796.[5]

Still more spectacular was the rate of demographic expansion that took place in the Americas and along Russia's steppe frontier. In some Ukrainian districts, for example, population tripled in the eighteenth century through a combination of immigration and natural increase. In the Americas modest immigration from Europe continued throughout the eighteenth century, but spectacular rates of natural increase accounted for most of the expansion of the white population. The population of the English mainland colonies in North America, for example, grew from about 350,000 in 1700 to no less than 5 million in 1800![6] More interesting, perhaps, is the fact that the die-off of Indian peoples, which had been such an important factor in initial encounters between Old and New World populations, bottomed out about a century and a half after contacts were initiated. As a result, in Mexico and Peru Indian and mestizo populations began to grow rapidly by the last decades of the eighteenth century, and at a pace that soon equalled or exceeded the rate of white population growth.

Enslaved African populations were not self-sustaining in

tropical regions; in the mainland colonies of North America, on the other hand, population growth among slaves also set in during the eighteenth century at a rate not much inferior to that of the white population.[7] Die-off continued to destroy isolated Indian tribes whenever white men inaugurated contact with them—a process continuing into the twentieth century. But the initial catastrophe in the heavily populated regions of the New World had passed by 1700 or before. With this, new patterns of encounter began among the diverse ethnic groups of the New World—a process we today are still trying to get used to in the United States.

The global or nearly global disturbance to older population equilibria which manifested itself in the eighteenth century was a fundamental destabilizer of human affairs thereafter. Something over 90 percent of the earth's population lived by working the soil when the process began. Population growth therefore initially meant finding ways to accommodate young persons as they attained marriageable age within the framework of existing rural society. When adequate land lay close at hand and property rights did not interfere, a growing population simply meant expansion of tillage; and until that sort of internal colonization began to bring marginal lands under cultivation, local village living standards and styles of life did not need to alter very much.

When the eighteenth-century population growth set in, cultivable land *did* lie within easy reach of established village communities in most parts of the earth. This was generally the case in Latin America, for example, where earlier Amerindian die-off had emptied vast stretches of good land. Cultivable land was probably available in vast areas of India and Africa as well. The same was certainly true in eastern Europe, where peasant occupancy of the landscape remained comparatively thin. In these regions, therefore, the onset of the new demographic regime after 1750 made little difference at first. As each new generation came of age, new fields could be found for them to cultivate. Their presence enhanced the total wealth of society and sustained a continued growth of political and commercial networks. Often, from the peasants' point of view, there was a price to pay in the form of harsher subjection to landowners who could choose among competing bidders for access to land they controlled. But frictions over how to divide a growing total production were not very acute as long as new fields kept up with new mouths to feed.

In other regions of the earth, however, more drastic changes were triggered by the new population pattern. Wherever cultivators had already occupied almost all of the fertile soil, a hard choice confronted young people as they came of age. Either they could stay in place, with the prospect of inheriting only a share of their parents' holdings, or they could leave the familiar environment in which they had grown up, and seek a better future somewhere else.

When new crops and techniques were available, subdividing peasant holdings could proceed without putting such a strain on older living standards and expectations as to be unacceptable. This seems to have happened in much of China, for example, as well as in some regions of western Europe. In Java this pattern went to unparalleled extremes, thanks to the remarkable responsiveness of paddy fields to intensified labor inputs, and to a social system that "developed into a dense web of finely spun work rights and work responsibilities spread, like the reticulate veins of the hand, throughout the whole body of the village lands."[8] Irish peasants, by exploiting the fact that a single acre of potatoes could feed an entire family, did much the same before the catastrophic potato famine hit in 1845-1847, while at the other end of Europe, Rumanian peasants came to depend on the other great American staple, maize, so completely as to become liable to pellagra. No doubt other rural communities, e.g., in India and Japan, also responded to growing population by what Clifford Geertz aptly christened "agricultural involution."

A second and in many ways more successful, because more elastic, response to population pressure on the land was to go in for handicraft manufacture. This allowed extra hands to survive in the village by supplementing agricultural with industrial sources of income. Assuredly, wherever villages were already in contact with a commercial network, rising rural populations put serious new pressures on guild and other urban manufacturing monopolies. In many parts of Europe, rural industry was already centuries old. It dated back, largely, to an earlier age of population crunch when, before the Black Death, the peasants of England, the Low Countries, and adjacent parts of Europe broke through urban monopolies by going in for the manufacture of cheap textiles. This pattern intensified in the eighteenth century and spread to new ground, e.g., to Ulster and Silesia, where linen-weaving began to sustain dense, poverty-stricken multitudes.

But for us, trying to understand what transpired along the frontiers of an expanding European world, what mattered most was the alternative to domestic manufacture and/or agricultural involution, i.e., migration.

The easiest kind of migration was short-range: from village to town. Such a flow was as old as civilization itself, because towns and cities were places of demographic decay due to intensified infection. Until modern sewage systems and other public health measures took effect in the second half of the nineteenth century, urban populations could not sustain themselves biologically without recruitment from the healthier countryside. But the systematically accelerated influx beginning to descend upon the towns of western Europe in the last decades of the eighteenth century, created immediate problems. No adequate livelihood automatically offered itself for the flood of newcomers.

One response was riot and protest. In France this allowed the dynamic of the French Revolution to run its remarkable course. Domestic riot and constitutional upheaval gave way after 1792 to civil and foreign war; and the emergency of 1793 occasioned the famous *levée en masse* whereby otherwise underemployed young men were recruited into the army. This proved an efficacious way of relieving population pressure in France. Army deaths very nearly equalled natural increase in the years of Napoleon's campaigns. Demobilization in 1815 had another unexpected by-product, for methods of birth control (perhaps propagated by army experiences of sex) became sufficiently widespread in postwar France to affect the further growth of population in that country. This distinguished France from adjacent parts of Europe, where far higher rates of natural increase continued to prevail until near the end of the century.

More important for the world as a whole was the eighteenth-century response of Great Britain to the accelerated urban influx of employable young people. A generation of expert study of the causes of the commercial and industrial changes that began to assume revolutionary proportions in Great Britain after about 1780 now seems to have reached consensus about the centrality of population growth in provoking the Industrial Revolution.[9] The role of population pressure in precipitating the political and military upheavals of the French Revolution and Napoleonic Wars is far less firmly grounded in existing historiography, but will, I think, soon become a cliché of European history if ideological pieties do not interfere.[10]

As we all know, once the shocks of the Napoleonic Wars

had passed, the industrial and commercial transformation of European society gained momentum and began to spread beyond British borders. New technology soon improved transportation fundamentally: first steamships, then railroads. Older limits on movement of men and commodities were left far behind as fossil fuels enlarged the energies that human beings could call upon at will. The result was to facilitate movement to and fro within an expanding Europe-centered world system, and to project an ever-larger number of disease-experienced persons into remote corners of the earth, where their encounters with previously isolated communities promoted die-offs and created vast new frontiers for Europeans to develop. South Africa, Australia, and Oceania were thereby added to North and South America as theaters for European settlement; and rapidly growing populations in the densely occupied parts of western (and ere long of central and eastern) Europe provided a stock of would-be migrants, whenever obstacles of cost and ignorance of the unknown could be overcome.

How, then, were these new dynamics of human ecology registered along the frontiers? What happened to the older antithetical complementarity between egalitarian anarchy and legally enforced subordination? Needless to say, each place and time was different. Variability, reaching down to the roles of individuals in particular actions and situations, was infinite. This dimension of the historical past ought not to be swept under the rug by attempts such as mine to look at the broad picture, searching for patterns of such generality as to lose touch with individual and local uniqueness. General and particular genuinely coexist, and when accurately discerned are equally true. Anyone who has looked at a landscape from the top of a tall building or from an airplane as well as from the ground will surely believe this to be so. With this nod to the microhistorical approach to reality, let me climb back into orbit and try to answer the question: What difference did the post-1750 demographic regime make along Europe's far-flung frontiers?

Overall and in the long run, the effect of demographic growth and cheapened transport after 1750 was to reduce differences between center and periphery. But this took time, and whenever a newly emptied frontier opened, the initial stark contrast between freedom and hierarchy reappeared, sometimes briefly, sometimes enduring down to the present. In Australia, for example, the contrast between the lawless bushrangers of the Outback and the prison regimen imposed on the convict labor supplied to New South Wales between 1788 and 1840 was as stark as the contrast between New World slavery and freedom—and a good deal more violent.[11]

In South Africa too, the Boers, who successfully pioneered a mainly pastoral style of life on the veld during the course of the eighteenth century, enslaved the native Hottentots, whose vulnerability to imported diseases resembled that of other isolated populations. When, however, Boer pioneers collided with Bantu-speaking "kaffirs" the terms of epidemiological encounter altered, inasmuch as the Bantu were about as disease-experienced as the Dutch, and enjoyed much the same technological and epidemiological superiority over Hottentots as did the Boers.

The superiority of gun to spear therefore became decisive along the frontier where these two expanding peoples met, clashing for the first time in 1702. Repeated bloody encounters set in during the 1770s, and lasted for a full century. (The Zulu war of 1879 was the last major struggle.) At stake was the right to land and access to water holes. Whatever whites prevailed they took possession of the good land. African tribal society retreated into refuge areas, where agriculture was precarious owing to recurrent droughts. But the land the Boers appropriated was not completely cleared of kaffirs. Individuals and families left behind when the tribes went down in defeat were put to work by the new landowners, who thereby escaped the indignity of manual labor. Forms of engagement differed from the convict labor of Australia, but the reality of compulsion backed by legal forms and military force was not fundamentally different.

Yet among themselves the Boers were stubbornly egalitarian and anarchic. As free men they clashed repeatedly with British officials' efforts after 1805 to introduce regular administration, protect native rights, and impose taxes. Hence frontier freedom and hierarchy coexisted in South Africa in a peculiarly intense fashion that persists down to our own time.[12]

Between 1750 and 1850, therefore, Australia and South Africa recapitulated, with variations of their own, the familiar frontier pattern of sharp social polarization. Nor did similar polarities disappear from the Americas. They were in fact reborn with every new advance of the frontier from the first zones of encounter. Thus, for example, Brazilian sugar plantations, based on slavery and usually situated fairly near the coast, were supplemented in the eighteenth century by important inland mines where enslaved Negroes and Indians provided much of the labor for digging gold and diamonds from the ground. But, like the Boers of South Africa, the most inveterate Brazilian pioneers, the Paulistas, were themselves belligerently egalitarian and all but ungovernable, save when they voluntarily formed themselves into quasi-military bands for ventures deep into the interior. Their exploration and slave raiding expanded Brazil's territory deep into the hinterland, and provoked a long series of clashes with Spaniards and other European rivals. Runaway slaves were also able to form a polity of their own in the Brazilian backwoods, but between 1772 and 1794 Paulista *bandierantes* destroyed this rival to their dominion by persistent armed attacks.[13]

In North America, slave plantations in Alabama, Mississippi, and east Texas shared in the frontier movement across the continent until 1865. And, at the libertarian extreme, free and equal agricultural pioneers living in isolated cabins were matched by the competitive anarchy of pioneer gold miners in California and Colorado, and the counter-culture of such specialized frontier populations as the buffalo-hunting *metis* of Manitoba, whose armed collision with Canadian authorities in 1885 has become part of French Canadian hagiography.[14]

An important variant of frontier patterns of life, deliberately omitted from my first lecture, was illustrated anew by the Mormon trek to Utah in 1846-1847. Brigham Young and the eleven other Apostles of the new faith replicated in essentials what the Pilgrim Fathers of Massachusetts had achieved some two centuries before. For, like the Puritan leaders of the seventeenth century, Mormon church authorities managed to impose a stern discipline upon their followers. This, in turn, allowed them to transplant a tight-knit community, numbering thousands, from Illinois to Utah. Far-ranging, quasi-military subordination of ordinary believers to church authorities made the feat possible. Yet obedience in all the strenuous shared labors of building Zion in the wilderness was freely rendered in nearly every case.

The Mormons' remarkable social discipline was sustained by the fact that irrigation agriculture, upon which the main body came to depend, required common effort and centralized control. Isolated households could not hope to achieve comparable success in harnessing the streams descending from the mountains into the desert basin of Utah. Thus the technical conditions of life in the new community sustained and

[42]

reinforced the religious bonds that made large-scale exploitation of water resources possible in the first place.[15]

In this respect, the Mormons were more fortunate than their Puritan forerunners, for the subsistence farming of New England, conducted by independent nuclear families, benefited only marginally from any kind of collective effort and therefore remained technically quite independent of public authority. For that reason, perhaps, the theocracy of Massachusetts did not endure for as long as a century, whereas the Latter-Day Saints of Jesus Christ, to give the Mormons their proper name, continue to flourish and still manage to maintain remarkable cohesiveness, despite the clashes with federal authorities in the last decades of the nineteenth century that resulted in dismantlement of the collective polity that Brigham Young had erected.

Sectarian communities organized and disciplined by religious faith and subordinated to ecclesiastical leaders also flourished along the Russian frontier. Some were foreign, like the German Mennonites who succeeded in setting up prosperous agricultural communities along the banks of the Don and Volga in the eighteenth century. More important for Russia as a whole were dissidents within the Orthodox faith itself, the so-called Old Believers. Persecution by Russian churchmen drove many of the Old Believers toward remote forests and marginal steppelands where the writ of the Russian government ceased to run. In the north, refugees from persecution succeeded in setting up some remarkable communities that supplemented what they could raise and gather from infertile soils with manufacture of ironware and other handicrafts. They also devised a surprisingly elaborate, far-ranging trade system so as to be able to bring back enough grain to make good the shortfall of their own harvests. As a result, Old Believers became pioneers of Russian industry and commerce in quite disproportionate degree.

Official persecution relaxed in the eighteenth century only to intensify anew in the twentieth. As a result, some of the Russian Mennonites and Old Believers found it prudent to colonize selected spots along the American frontier, scattering themselves all the way from Argentina and Paraguay in the south to the United States and Canada in the north. In the New World these sects soon replicated, though in somewhat softened form, the collisions with constituted authority that had so often distinguished them in Russia.[16]

Frontier sectarianism could also assume more grisly form. In South Africa, for example, Bantu tribesmen slaughtered their cattle and consumed their seed corn in 1857 on the strength of a religious revelation that promised spiritual replenishment of the land and its purgation of whites. Mass starvation ensued.[17] In Brazil, a generation later, a millenarian cult formed around a wild holy man who was called "Good Jesus Comforter" by his followers. They took to arms and soon provoked war to the death with state authorities. After two years of fighting the struggle ended in 1897 with the total massacre of the defiant believers.[18] More recently, in 1978, the mass suicide of Jim Jones's followers, who had gone pioneering in the hostile environment of the Guyana rain forest, shocked American public opinion with a macabre exhibition of how far a search for freedom through voluntary submission to religious authority can go. Such (only seemingly) paradoxical behavior has always been peculiarly at home along the frontier. There men are few so that scoffing unbelievers cannot do much to threaten the community of the faithful, whereas cooperative effort, sustained by common belief, permits practical achievements far beyond anything isolated pioneer families can accomplish by themselves.

In these and other instances, frontier society in Eurasia and the Americas continued to exhibit the tension between op-posites that is characteristic of regions where land abounds while people and skills are in short supply. Anarchic freedom and artificially reinforced social hierarchy continued to mix like fire and water throughout the moving frontier zones of the earth after, as well as before, 1750.

The new element in east European and in American society that assumed growing importance after the middle of the eighteenth century was characteristic, instead, of our effete east. For along the Atlantic coast of this country, at the centers of political management in Latin America and in cities of the Ukraine, Rumania, and Hungary, complexly stratified social structures approximating more and more closely to west European patterns began to flourish. Philadelphia, New York and Boston, Budapest, Bucharest and Kiev, Mexico City, Lima and Buenos Aires—to name but a few of the key centers—began to play the role of metropolis to their respective hinterlands more and more adequately as population grew and skills increased. Occupational differentiation like that of European cities proliferated. Varying wage rates became capable of apportioning labor among competing occupations more and more effectively. Severe legal penalties for changing jobs no longer were necessary to get nasty tasks done. Serfdom and slavery therefore became dispensable, though a century and more passed before the law fully ratified this changing social reality.

The American War of Independence and the establishment of a new sovereign government on American soil (1776-1789) hastened the process of transferring the full panoply of European civilization to the New World. Latin America lagged only slightly behind, for Spain's American empire was reduced to a few tattered fragments between 1808 and 1821, and Brazil also became independent in 1822, though it remained under the rule of a branch of the Portuguese royal house until 1889.

Self-government and all the trappings of sovereignty generated new occupations and a new spirit as well. But exact replication of Europe was never in question. If nothing else, race mixture in the Americas guaranteed enduring differences. Relations between Amerindian or largely Amerindian segments of the population and descendants of European and African immigrants worked themselves out in varying ways in different parts of the New World. In Haiti, blacks displaced all others; in New England whites did the same. But in most regions black, white, and red shared the ground in varying proportions with an ever-rising number of persons of mixed blood.

As long as fresh land could readily be found for youths reaching marriageable age, population growth presented no really critical problems. In the United States and Canada, the politically volatile issues everywhere turned on relations between urban centers, where the new managerial elites concentrated, and rural folk. In remoter parts of Latin America, Amerindian villagers continued to pursue a subsistence pattern of life almost unaffected by outsiders; but in central Mexico and other regions closer to urban markets and political seats of power, disruptive intervention of the market and of individuals with access to legal devices for extending their control over land divided society into hostile and more or less uncomprehending rival camps.

But even in such cases, the long-term effect of improved transportation and communications—the railroad, telegraph, newspaper, and all their twentieth-century equivalents—was to narrow the gap between town and country by enlarging the scale of market transactions in rural life. Galloping commercialization, in turn, generated political frictions, because the rural partners felt aggrieved by unfavorable terms of trade. The upshot, overall, was to bring erstwhile frontier societies closer to the European metropolitan pattern and at a relatively rapid rate.

Perhaps the most obvious register of the diminishing difference between the social structures of the European center and the frontier societies of the earth was the legal abolition of serfdom and slavery that occurred during the nineteenth century. This was a step-by-step process of course, since different sovereignties held jurisdiction. The earliest landmark was the prohibition of slavery within Great Britain in 1772, achieved by judicial interpretation rather than through formal legislation. Beginning with Vermont in 1777, some states within the new American union prohibited slavery by formal legislation, and so did the French revolutionary Convention in 1794. The Convention's act affected French possessions overseas, most notably Haiti, where a bloody insurrection was required to prevent Napoleon from reinstating slavery. Next, slavery was abolished throughout the British empire in 1833 by Act of Parliament. Thereafter the Royal Navy attempted to police the seas in order to intercept slave ships. Within two decades the Atlantic trade in slaves had been effectively halted; but not until the 1890s did slaving on Africa's east coast come completely to an end.

Only in the United States did the abolition of slavery involve large-scale resort to armed force. The Civil War (1861-1865) may not have turned solely on slavery, but surely that was the central issue throughout.[19] Thereafter, Brazil remained the principal slaveholding country in the Americas. Abolition came there peaceably in 1888. Ten years later, after the British had intervened in Zanzibar to stop that island from exporting slaves to Arab lands, African slavery became only a memory.

[47]

On Europe's eastern flank parallel legal changes took place during the same decades. The serfdom that had been instituted in the fifteenth, sixteenth, and seventeenth centuries to attach labor to the soil, so that landowners could increase their export of grain to western markets, was dismantled in the course of the nineteenth century. The process began when Prussia's defeat at Jena (1806) provoked reformers to abolish serfdom as part of that country's program of regeneration. A second wave of revolutionary reform led to the elimination of obligatory labor throughout the Hapsburg empire in 1848. Russia followed suit in 1861, and the last surviving bastion of serfdom disappeared from European soil in 1864 when Rumania did likewise.[20]

The end of these legal systems sanctioning compulsory labor outside and beyond market-regulated contracts did much to narrow the gap between frontier societies and the social structures at the centers of European civilization. But peonage remained important in Mexico and other parts of Latin America until the twentieth century, and contract labor, entered into by human beings who lacked familiarity with European law and custom, often resembled slavery very closely. It is therefore a mistake to suppose that legally sanctioned compulsory labor disappeared with the abolition of serfdom and slavery.

Australian history illustrates this very clearly. The last convicts were sent from Britain to Australia in 1867, cutting off the supply of prisoners' labor that had hitherto played a considerable role in getting things done "down under." Labor-short sugar plantations in Queensland thereupon met their problem by importing indentured laborers from the Solomon Islands under conditions approximating slavery. But the grant of self-government to the Australian colonies in 1850 had the effect of obstructing wholesale resort to indentured labor and

[48]

assured that a "white Australia" policy would prevail. Chinese coolie immigration, begun at the time of the Australian gold rush in 1851, was stopped by legislative action in 1855, for example; and permanent residence was rigorously denied to the "kanakas" who continued to work on sugar plantations in the north.

The activities of the Belgian King Leopold's agents in the Congo, which became an international scandal in the first decade of this century, offer a better-known example of how compulsory labor could be prolonged beyond the time when legal prohibition of slavery had been written into European law and opinion. In South Africa, too, what amounted to compulsory labor survived by assuming new legal forms after the 1860s, when the discovery of gold and diamonds put sudden new pressures on older social and political patterns. Technical requirements for deep-rock mining dictated large-scale corporate organization; but the resulting super-modern style of business management proved compatible with a radically discriminatory labor system that paid high wages to unionized white miners and kept black African wages low. This was possible because the breakdown of tribal discipline combined with population pressure in the native reserves to create an African labor force that in practice had to accept almost any terms of employment the mining companies offered. South Africa therefore maintained into the last decades of the twentieth century an exploitative system of labor whose equivalent had disappeared almost everywhere else.[21]

But, for all their notoriety, exploitative labor contracts in South Africa and the Congo were statistically less important than the global deployment of Indian indentured labor, both within India and in various remote tropical regions of the globe. There is, indeed, some irony in the fact that the abolition of slavery throughout the British empire in 1833 set the

[49]

scene for a vast increase in the employment of "coolie" labor to perform all the tasks that could not be accomplished by reliance on some more locally available work force. Indentured Indians in effect replaced enslaved Africans wherever British (and sometimes French) enterprise needed extra hands in tropical lands.

Within India itself, the coolie labor system sustained a continued frontier expansion. For, beginning in the 1840s and continuing until the 1920s, when the pressure of Indian public opinion led to the abolition of the system, tea plantations employed coolies to penetrate the virgin jungles of Assam in the best frontier tradition. Planters recruited their labor from crowded Indian villages by offering five-year indentures. Consequently, in the decade 1911-1921, when tea production in Assam reached its height, no fewer than 769,000 Indians were imported to that province under conditions that amounted to slavery. Actual working conditions on the tea plantations may in fact have been harsher than most forms of slavery, for the employers had no long-term stake in keeping their work force healthy; and the warm, wet climate allowed a formidable array of tropical diseases to afflict the imported workers.[22]

Elsewhere in the British empire, in Mauritius, Trinidad, Ceylon, Natal, etc., indentured laborers from India also played an important role in the nineteenth and early twentieth centuries. Altogether, 27.7 million Indians left the country between 1835 and 1920, nearly all of them as members of coolie gangs. About 24 million returned at the expiration of their contracts. Most of the remainder died, but a few lived on and their descendants constitute a distinct element in the local populations to the present.[23] Comparable statistics from China do not exist, but Chinese coolies were far fewer. Nonetheless, Chinese indentured laborers played a prominent part in the Australian gold rush (1851-1856), and gangs of Chinese coolies dug guano in Peru (1840s-1870s) and built the first railroads in California (1860s) and western Canada (1880s). Australia's "whites only" policy meant that all the Chinese had to go home; but in North America some remained behind when their work contracts expired, thus starting up the well-known Chinese communities of San Francisco and Vancouver.

The survival of thinly disguised forms of compulsion for mustering labor on the fringes of European expansion should not surprise us. There was no other way that the sugar industry could continue to thrive, or that railroad building and other large-scale construction projects could be carried through in places where local populations were scant or felt no incentive to alter their accustomed ways of life to work for white intruders. Moreover, the process fed on itself. Dock and railroad construction in remote places opened new possibilities for profitable mining and plantation enterprises, provided that a suitable work force could be brought to the scene. Coolies served the purpose as well or better than slaves could have done, since the temporary character of the engagement and the vestigial voluntarism of signing on made hard conditions seem both morally defensible to employers and bearable to the workers.

Yet, even though coolie labor became a really big business and carried nearly three times as many persons across the world's oceans as ever left Africa in Atlantic slave ships, legally sanctioned compulsion as a way of getting things done was nonetheless a diminishing, retreating mode of labor organization in the nineteenth and twentieth centuries. This was so because enslaved and indentured labor was dwarfed by a mass migration from Europe that set in after 1840.

Earlier migrations of free men from Europe went largely unrecorded, but by the time this mass movement got underway the diligence of modern governments resulted in the collection of relatively exact figures. We therefore know that about 46.2 million Europeans took up residence overseas between 1846 and 1920. More than 10 million others pioneered eastward in Siberia and the Caucasus lands during the latter part of that same period—mainly between 1880 and 1914.[24] Transoceanic movement of coolie labor amounted to about half as much during the same period of time. Free labor thus overbalanced compulsory labor decisively in the continuing economic development of European frontier and ex-frontier lands after the middle of the nineteenth century; whereas, as we saw in the first lecture, before 1800 the balance tilted quite the other way, since African slaves far outnumbered Europeans among immigrants to the Americas; and a large proportion of the Europeans who crossed the ocean did so as unfree indentured servants.

The brief extraordinary surge (1840-1920) of freely undertaken long-distance migration, financed individually or within small kinship groups, was a remarkable phenomenon in world history, and quite without parallel. It bulks so large in the national consciousness of the United States that many people assume it to be the normal form of human migration. But this is profoundly erroneous. Migrations that mattered, i.e., those that were successful in transplanting a population to new ground, have nearly always been conducted by organized groups, armed and prepared to repel the natives whose land they proposed to take over. The Biblical account of winning the Promised Land is therefore a far better model for the history of human migration than the pattern that prevailed in the nineteenth and twentieth centuries.

Individual and familial management of what became a mass movement was, indeed, so exceptional as to require special explanation. We can discern four unusual circumstances that came together to permit so vast an outpouring. First, steamships (from the 1840s) and then railroads (from the 1850s) made long-distance travel cheaper, faster, and far more capacious than before. Simultaneously, improved communications made reasonably accurate information available in European towns and villages about attractive conditions of life overseas or along the Siberian railroad. Thirdly, receiving lands welcomed newcomers because local managerial elites realized that immigrant labor would accelerate economic growth of a kind that they and nearly everyone else on the scene could expect to benefit from. Finally, a widespread population crunch in European villages supplied millions of young persons who were willing to seek their fortunes in distant lands because nothing satisfactory seemed possible at home.

As I remarked before, during the eighteenth century, when the modern population surge first began to affect Europe, in most places extra young people could make a satisfactory living simply by clearing new fields from waste and pasture lands lying close by. After the middle of the nineteenth century, however, in more and more parts of Europe, this simple response to rising numbers became impractical because all readily cultivable land had been taken up. Emigration therefore offered an obvious and increasingly accessible escape from an otherwise desperate *cul-de-sac*.

Of course, long-distance migration remained expensive even when steamships and railroads had done all they could to reduce transport costs. Millions of European peasants overcame this obstacle by using kinship ties to create and sustain a flow of migration from their overcrowded villages to hospitable communities overseas. Initial lodgment was always difficult and problematic. Exceptional individual enterprise or some unusual concatenation of circumstance was often necessary to plant the first emigrant from a given village in a distant and propitious spot where he could prosper. But when that occurred, the prospering newcomer, whether in the United States, Canada, Argentina, Australia, or somewhere else, commonly sent money back home in order to bring close relatives to wherever he had set himself up. Each newly arrived person could then do likewise, creating a chain of migration that might endure for several generations. Such arrangements allowed a large number of European villages to establish overseas extensions of the home community that sometimes far outnumbered those remaining behind. After the 1880s, when good agricultural land had nearly all been occupied overseas, these immigrant communities congregated in cities for the most part. Yet even in such radically alien environments village, regional, and especially religious ties from the old country allowed the migrants to retain a sense of collective identity and social control, at least for the first generation.

Not all of the Europeans who crossed the oceans after 1840 did so as fully free persons. Some depended on employers or labor contractors to pay their fares, and arrived at their destinations with the legal obligation to pay back the sums advanced, usually by agreeing to work for the person who had financed the passage. Like the contractors who provided Indian coolie labor in the tropics, bosses who recruited European manpower for remote mining and construction enterprises in temperate zones were not overscrupulous in their treatment of the people they carried across the sea. One of my own ancestors, for example, was shipped round the Horn to Vancouver Island sometime in the 1860s to mine coal for the Royal Navy; and if oral tradition is to be trusted, the conditions of life he left behind in Scotland and those he met with in British Columbia were about equally grim.

All the same, the enhanced possibility for voluntary emigration that set in after 1840 clearly tipped the balance between freedom and compulsion as the predominant mode of organizing work throughout the far-flung frontier lands open to European settlement. The influx of Irish and German, and then of Italian and Slavic immigrants, supplementing a continued flow from Great Britain itself, confirmed and expanded the predominance within the United States of market relationships and individual freedom as the way of staffing any and every sort of enterprise, large or small, public or private. Resulting rapid economic growth more than justified the abolition of slavery in 1863.[25] Chile, Brazil, and Argentina, together with Australia, New Zealand, Canada, and South Africa, became other important receivers of the swarming Europeans. In these countries, too (with the partial exception of South Africa and after the final abolition of slavery in Brazil in 1888) free choice of employment prevailed within limits set by a market operating with remarkably little legal restriction.

There was a catch to the new weight that individual choice and private decision-making came to have in peopling the frontiers of the earth. Some European villages (in south Italy, for example) were devitalized and well-nigh destroyed by losing too many of their inhabitants to America before 1914. Moreover, in the new lands to which the emigrants went, inequities and exploitation of the weak by the strong played variously ugly roles. Settlers eager to set up as farmers or in some other occupation within easy reach of the new railroads did not escape intimate involvement in the worldwide commercial network that sustained European civilization, nor did they wish to do so. But inasmuch as their new life depended on large-scale buying and selling, these latter-day pioneers found themselves very much at the mercy of middlemen who controlled the movement of goods to and from the regions where they had located.

[55]

Clashes of interest were built into this situation. Consequently, populist protest in the United States and comparable movements based in the hinterlands of other frontier countries played a very prominent part in late nineteenth- and early twentieth-century politics. Not until World War I did the gap between commercial and rural occupations and ways of life begin to narrow in the United States, as farmers became more urbanized in outlook and began to treat farming as a business. In Canada, Australia, New Zealand, and Argentina the commercialization of agriculture moved more or less *pari passu* with the transformation of rural life in the United States. The frontier heritage of differentiation and distrust between center and periphery faded proportionately.

After World War II even the ambivalences between freedom and compulsion characteristic of company towns at remote mining sites diminished markedly. Military experience in managing troops stationed at isolated outposts provided a model and standard for postwar civilian enterprise. As a result, since the 1950s miners and construction workers, even when employed at the ends of the earth, in remote Arctic locations or on deserts of the Persian Gulf, could fly in and out at frequent intervals. Such workers therefore kept effectively in touch with a larger world where free markets were more of a reality than could ever be the case in places where there was only one employer and only one supplier of outside goods.[26]

Recent developments within the vast reaches of the Russian empire also narrowed the gap between rural and urban, agricultural and industrial, ways of life. But in an interesting sense, in Russia it was the rural rather than the urban element that predominated in the amalgam.

The role of the market and of individual choice always remained slender in the Russian lands. Even after the abolition of serfdom in 1861, free contracts and a privately operated market in goods and services had only a comparatively modest development in Russia. Governmental decisions and bureaucratic initiatives mattered far more than in western countries, both before and after 1917. The Russian Revolution had the effect of enhancing the role of compulsion once more. War, communism (1917-1921), and the Five Year plans that started in 1928 mustered the labor force required for military and industrial undertakings by the old-fashioned method of issuing commands, backed by the threat and sometimes by the exercise of force. The change was most dramatically registered on the far margins of Russian society, where pioneering in the harsh climate of Siberia came to depend almost wholly on convict labor, directed by the secret police.

But lest we congratulate ourselves too warmly on the newly conspicuous gap between Soviet compulsion and our own greater reliance or private response to market incentives, let me conclude by pointing out that since the 1880s American society, too, has come increasingly under the influence of bureaucratic management. At first it was the bureaucracies of private corporations that mattered most.[27] But since the 1930s, governmental bureaucrats, allied with labor and business bureaucrats, have taken over primacy in regulating the lives of nearly all United States citizens.

No doubt, indirect controls of the sort favored in the United States are less galling than overt compulsion, but they are not altogether different either. A complex, differentiated, flow-through economy, staffed by diverse ethnic and religious groups who are united more by propinquity than by any obvious cultural uniformity, probably requires management by some kind of power elite. Certainly, traditional empires in the deeper past were managed in that way. The world market of the eighteenth and nineteenth centuries was also managed in important degree by a small number of bankers, merchants, politicians, and officials, nearly all of whom were based in western Europe. Indeed, the price of complete personal freedom is to consume only what one can produce for oneself in a place where risk of armed attack by outsiders has somehow been effectually exorcised. Such places are far and few in our world; and the actual cost in material terms of withdrawal from dependence on market relations for the supply of human wants is far more than even the most incandescent rebels of the 1960s were willing to pay.

· · ·

THE history of the Great Frontier, as I see it, shows that the rewards of interdependence and exchange are too great to be foregone. But interdependence implies social hierarchy and management based on some mix of compulsion and incentive. Frontiersmen of the past acknowledged these realities, however begrudgingly, by their acts. None, or almost none, severed connection entirely with the civilized body whence they derived their skills and knowledge. They depended on supply from the rear for weapons and tools; and when improved communications in the nineteenth century established closer connections with civilized centers, few resisted the advantages which a broadened participation in market transactions offered, even when the terms of trade seemed systematically unfair.

The history of the United States, like the history of other lands brought within the circle of western European civilization in the past four hundred years, clearly registers these preferences. On an even grander scale, the history of humanity across the past five thousand years attests to the advantages of membership in civilized society, despite inherent inequalities and all the constraints on freedom that such membership entails.

Measured against such a time scale, the frontier phenomenon with which we have here been concerned appears as a remarkable but transitory wound, arising as a result of a demographic and cultural catastrophe to the normal equilibrium of the human ecosystem. Signs that the regimen of the past five hundred years is at an end are not wanting. For the process through which Europeans created the Great Frontier and occupied so many lands wound down very fast after 1914. World War I interrupted the flood of European emigration, and during the 1920s quota systems imposed by receiving countries prevented resumption of migration on the prewar scale.

Instead, changes in European family patterns and sex habits lowered the birth rate. As a result, except for Albanians, European peoples after World War II no longer nurtured large numbers of children who, on attaining adulthood, were unable to find satisfactory careers at home. Instead, when economic boom set in during the 1950s, migration started to run in an opposite direction, bringing millions of Moslems into the old heartlands of European civilization. As a result, Pakistanis in Britain, Algerians in France, Turks in West Germany, and several different ethnic strands of Central Asian and Caucasus Moslems in the Soviet Union began to staff the unattractive jobs in each country.

It is interesting to observe how the ancient nations of Europe thus came to resemble overseas lands of settlement more closely than before. For since World War II the principal cities of Europe have become polyethnic, just like American, Australian, and South African cities. The gap between center and periphery thereby narrowed still more. But this time the gap was closed not by bringing the peripheral lands nearer to European norms, but by altering the social pattern of Europe itself.

Such a reversal surely attests to the completion of a process of European expansion that dominated the world for about four and a half centuries after 1500. We now can say that the movement outward from Europe of peoples, institutions, skills, and ideas which generated the Great Frontier seems finally to have come to a halt. What new movements may take its place, time will tell. It would be naive to suppose that changes in the terms of encounter among the major branches of humanity have finally achieved a lasting equilibrium. On the contrary, flux and reflux seem likely to intensify as communications become ever denser and transport capacity expands. But the drastically one-sided character of cultural encounter that prevailed across the Great Frontier seems unlikely to recur. Only some apocalyptic disaster leading to the sudden depopulation of large parts of the earth could reproduce the frontier circumstances of the recent past.

We can discern a natural succession for the repair of the demographic catastrophe that beset disease-vulnerable populations in early modern times. European pioneering was the principal expression of that process. Each successive stage of frontier life, as analyzed nearly a century ago by Turner, established greater social complexity and a more subtly graded social hierarchy, thereby repairing the initial rent in the human occupancy of the earth.

Idealization of one or another of the stages of development toward a more fully civilized condition is a kind of romantic delusion to which both Turner and Webb, along with a large segment of the American public, were susceptible.[28] But by now the United States has come fully abreast of the old centers of European civilization in most respects. It is time our historiography caught up, and ceased to glorify a parochial past, recognizing instead our place in the grand epos of European civilization, and of the whole human adventure on earth.

This, it seems to me, is the beginning of wisdom. To put

our country back into the world from which, in truth, it never departed, even in the most isolationist decades of the nineteenth century, is the most urgent task before historians in the United States. Perhaps these lectures may provoke others to make the attempt, in order to improve details and correct the perspectives I have been able to bring to the task.

Notes

LECTURE I

1. Frederick Jackson Turner, *The Frontier in American History* (New York, 1920), p. 4. This book is a reprint of Turner's essays.

2. Ibid., p. 23.

3. Ibid., p. 37.

4. Ibid., p. 37.

5. Margaret Walsh, *The American Frontier Revisited* (Atlantic Highlands, N.J., 1981), summarizes recent debate; Ray Allen Billington, *The American Frontier Thesis: Attack and Defense*, rev. ed. (Washington, D.C., 1971), remains, however the best survey of the subject, offering a magistral and judicious, though firmly pious, treatment of Turnerian historiography.

6. Walter Webb, *The Great Frontier* (New York, 1952). The idea for this book dated back to 1936, and matured in graduate seminars subsequently. Cf. Necah Stewart Furman, *Walter Prescott Webb: His Life and Impact* (Albuquerque, 1976), p. 108.

7. His friends established an annual Walter Webb Memorial lecture series at the University of Texas, Arlington, from which two books relevant to my theme resulted: *Essays on Walter Prescott Webb*, The Walter Prescott Webb Memorial Lectures, X (Austin, 1976), and George Wolfskill and Stanley Palmer, eds., *Essays on Frontier History* (Austin, 1981).

8. The enterprise was analogous to Turner's effort to emancipate U.S. history from thralldom to Europe and was pursued with the same obdurate provincialism, emphasizing autochthonous traditions and denying or minimizing external, especially European, impacts and global connections.

The same climate of opinion reinforced from a quite different quarter by narrow-minded political persecution, seems to have buried Owen Lattimore's elegant essay, "The Frontier in History." This was first presented to the Tenth International Congress of the Historical Sciences in 1955, and reprinted in Owen Lattimore, *Studies in Frontier History: Collected Essays, 1928-1958* (London, 1962), pp. 469-91. Lattimore's global vision anticipates my own in interesting ways, though I read his work only after completing these lectures and found no reason to change what I had said in the light of his remarks.

9. William H. McNeill, *The Rise of the West: A History of the Human Community* (Chicago, 1963), used this hypothesis to make sense of the world's history.

10. Nevertheless, both Europe and Japan were subjugated to invaders from the steppe very early in their history, and had to repel a Mongol threat at the apex of steppe military power in the thirteenth century.

11. James Lee, Ph.D. dissertation, University of Chicago, forthcoming, provides the best analysis of the centuries-long process of Chinese expansion, but cf. also Herold J. Wiens, *China's March Towards the Tropics* (Hamden, Conn., 1954).

12. On a smaller scale other rice-paddy societies shared Chinese powers of expansion. The Japanese moved north through their islands at the expense of the Ainu, for example, in much the same fashion as the Chinese went south; and within recent centuries rice-paddy fields spread across Java from a plurality of initial lodgments, supplanting slash-and-burn cultivation. Cf. Takane Matsuo, *Rice and Rice Cultivation in Japan* (Tokyo, 1961), pp. 1-2; Geertz, *Agricultural Involution: The Process of Ecological Change in Indonesia* (Berkeley and Los Angeles, 1966), pp. 38-46.

13. This reconstruction of events is by no means universally agreed upon. Russian plague experts assume that infection of the steppe rodents was age-old, and some western scholars accept this assumption for no good reason except that Russian authorities can be cited for the opinion. Arguments for the view here set forth can be found in William H. McNeill, *Plagues and Peoples* (New York, 1976), pp. 190-96.

14. For Russian northern expansion see Raymond H. Fisher, *The Russian Fur Trade, 1550-1770* (Berkeley, 1943).

15. William H. McNeill, *Plagues and Peoples*, pp. 199-216.

16. See the impassioned but epidemiologically uninformed account in Farley Mowat, *The Desperate People* (Boston, 1959).

17. Ralph A. Austin, "From the Atlantic to the Indian Ocean: European Abolition, the African Slave Trade, and Asian Economic Structures," in David Eltis and James Walvin, eds., *The Abolition of the Atlantic Slave Trade: Origins and Effects in Europe, Africa and the Americas* (Madison, Wis., 1981), p. 136, suggests that as many as 17

million Africans entered Islamic slavery between A.D. 650 and 1920. His efforts to estimate rates of traffic, spelled out in earlier articles cited in the above, suggest that rather more than half this total left their native communities after 1500. If these estimates are anywhere near right, the numbers of Africans crossing the Atlantic and the number crossing the Sahara and the Red Sea-Indian Ocean matched one another quite closely.

18. Drastic disorganization of traditional cultural values invited self-destructive escape into alcoholism among native peoples of the frontier. Cf. Mark Twain, *Life on the Mississippi*, ch. 60, "Speculations and Conclusions": "How solemn and beautiful is the thought that the earliest pioneer of civilization, the van-leader of civilization, is never the steamboat, never the railroad, never the newspaper, never the Sabbath-school, never the missionary—but always whisky! Such is the case. Look history over: you will see. The missionary comes after the whisky—I mean he arrives after the whisky has arrived; next comes the poor immigrant, with ax and hoe and rifle; next the trader; next the miscellaneous rush; next the gambler, desperado and highwayman, and all their kindred in sin of both sexes; and next the smart chap who has bought up an old grant that covers all the land; this brings the lawyer tribe; the vigilance committee brings the undertaker. All these interests bring the newspaper; the newspaper starts up politics and a railroad; all hands turn to and build a church and a jail—and behold! civilization is established forever in the land."

19. Stanley L. Engerman, "Servants to Slaves to Servants: Contract Labor and European Expansion" forthcoming in H. van den Boogaart and P. C. Emmer, eds., *Colonialism and Migration: Indentured Labour Before and After Slavery* (The Hague: Martinus Nijhoff/ Leiden University Press, Comparative Studies in Overseas History, Vol. VI).

20. David Eltis, "Free and Coerced Transatlantic Migrations: Some Comparisons," *American Historical Review*, forthcoming, Table 3 gives a grand total of 1,250,000 Europeans as emigrating to Brazil and Spanish America, excluding Peru, prior to 1825; but this total rests on a collocation of very flimsy estimates. Peter Boyd-Bowman, "The Regional Origins of the Earliest Spanish Colonists of America," *Modern Language Association Publications*, 71 (1956), 1152-72, calculates that 200,000 Spaniards reached America by 1600. James Lockhard, *Spanish Peru, 1532-1560* (Madison, 1968), p. 12, says that 8,000

Spaniards reach Peru within the first 25 years of the conquest. These were the only statistically careful estimates I found.

21. Engerman, *op.cit.*, p. 11. The landmark study was Philip Curtin, *The Atlantic Slave Trade: A Census* (Madison, 1969). Engerman's figure represents only minor modifications of Curtin's original calculations.

22. David W. Galenson, *White Servitude in Colonial America* (Cambridge, 1981), p. 17 and *passim*. I owe my chance to see Engerman's unpublished essay, cited above, to Professor Galenson's kindness in acting as intermediary.

23. Codfish were exceptional inasmuch as even small fishing ships could sail back to Europe at the end of the season and market their salted catch without any centralized management whatever.

24. Cf. Roger Mols, *Introduction à la démographie historique des villes d'Europe du XIVe au XVIIIe siècle*, 2 vols. (Louvain, 1955), for telling examples of the frequency and severity of local disease disasters in early modern centuries.

25. W.E.D. Allen, *The Ukraine: A History* (Cambridge, 1940), Boris Nolde, *La Formation de l'empire russe* (Paris, 1953), and William H. McNeill, *Europe's Steppe Frontier, 1500-1800* (Chicago, 1964), analyze this struggle.

LECTURE II

1. The landmark book is Emmanuel Le Roy Ladurie, *Times of Feast, Times of Famine: A History of Climate since the Year 1000* (New York, 1971).

2. No general history of the migration of American food crops exists. Berthold Laufer, *The American Plant Migration* I. *The Potato* (Chicago, 1938), projected such a work and wrote a preliminary essay on the potato before he died. With the exception of a few precocious places like Ireland, the eighteenth century was the time when the new crops became widespread—reflecting the close reciprocal relation between an enlarged labor force and increased food production.

3. This is the thesis of William H. McNeill, *Plagues and Peoples*, pp. 240-44. See also Emmanuel Le Roy Ladurie, "Un Concept: l'unification microbienne du monde (XIVe-XVIIe siècles)," *Revue suisse*

d'histoire, **23** (1973), 627-96. Michael W. Flinn, *The European Demographic System, 1500-1850* (Baltimore, 1981), offers an incisive summary of recent advances in demographic history. For what Flinn calls the eighteenth-century break-out from older equilibria, see pp. 76-101.

4. Ping-ti Ho, *Studies on the Population of China, 1368-1953* (Cambridge, Mass., 1959), p. 278.

5. Marcel R. Reinhard and André Armengaud, *Histoire générale de la population mondiale* (Paris, 1961), pp. 156, 180.

6. Reinhard and Armengaud, *op.cit.*, p. 205.

7. Robert W. Fogel and Stanley L. Engerman, *Time on the Cross: The Economics of American Negro Slavery* (Boston, 1974), pp. 25-29; Nicolas Sanchez-Albornoz, *The Population of Latin America: A History* (Berkeley and Los Angeles, 1974), pp. 86-145.

8. Clifford Geertz, *Agricultural Involution: The Process of Ecological Change in Indonesia* (Berkeley and Los Angeles, 1966), p. 99.

9. Phyllis Deane and W. A. Cole, *British Economic Growth, 1688-1959* (Cambridge, 1962), set forth the proposition authoritatively and W. A. Cole, "Eighteenth Century Economic Growth Revisited," *Explorations in Economic History* 10 (1973), pp. 327-48, reaffirmed his earlier conclusion a decade later. J. Habakkuk, *Population Growth and Economic Development since 1750* (New York, 1971), concurred.

10. On population and the French Revolution, see Oliven F. Hufton, *The Poor in Eighteenth Century France* (Oxford, 1974), and Y. LeMoigne, "Population et subsistance à Strassbourg au XVIIIe siècle" in M. Bouloiseau et al., *Contributions à l'histoire démographique de la révolution française* (Paris, 1962); W. H. McNeill, *The Pursuit of Power: Technology, Armed Force and Society since 1000* (Chicago, 1982), pp. 185-214.

11. Charles Manning Hope Clark, *A History of Australia*, 5 vols. (Melbourne, 1962-1978), is a standard authority. Cf. also H. C. Allen, *Bush and Backwoods: A Comparison of the Frontier in Australia and the United States* (Lansing, Mich., 1959).

12. Two fine books attest to recent American interest in comparison of our national frontier experience with that of South Africa: Howard Lamar and Leonard Thompson, eds., *The Frontier in History: North American and Southern African Compared* (New Haven, Conn., 1981) and George M. Frederickson, *White Supremacy: A Comparative Study in American and South African History* (New York,

1981). For a briefer but incisive analysis, cf. Leonard Thompson, "The Southern African Frontier in Comparative Perspective," in George Wolfskill and Stanley Palmer, eds., *Essays on Frontiers in World History* (Austin, Texas, 1981), pp. 86-120. For the early period, Richard Elphick and Hermann Giliomee, eds., *The Shaping of South African Society, 1652-1820* (Capetown, 1979), is especially remarkable for its ethnographic and geographical sensitivity. C. W. de Kiewit, *A History of South Africa: Social and Economic* (London, 1941), is still valuable, though Monica Wilson and Leonard Thompson, eds., *The Oxford History of South Africa*, 2 vols. (Oxford, 1969, 1971), is now a standard authority for South African history as a whole.

13. E. Bradford Burns, *A History of Brazil* (New York, 1970), pp. 42ff. Paulista *bandierantes*, Cossack hordes, and Boer commandos were strikingly similar frontier institutions. Each was constituted by a voluntary association of free men who, for a limited period of time, surrendered their ordinary liberty and submitted to military discipline under some chosen leader. Both Cossack hordes and Brazilian *bandierantes* were eventually annexed by their respective imperial governments; the Boer commandos, however, resisted any such taming by the English and instead turned against the imperial connection in 1880 and again in the Boer War of 1899-1902.

14. Hartwell Bowsfield, *Louis Riel: The Rebel and the Hero* (Toronto, 1971), tells the story.

15. The Mormons thus recapitulated the experience of the world's earliest civilizations. Religious authorities in the Tigris-Euphrates, Nile, and Indus valleys created a social hierarchy of unprecedented power and developed human skills as never before, all on a basis of irrigation agriculture that required large-scale pooling of labor for its maintenance. In exactly the same way, Brigham Young raised the Mormon community far above the level otherwise attainable by pioneers in the desert frontiers of North America. His early concentration of public resources on monumental temple-building aptly symbolizes this link with his remote predecessors, whose ziggurats and pyramids still astound us. Cf. Leonard J. Arrington, *Great Basin Kingdom: An Economic History of the Latter Day Saints, 1830-1900* (Cambridge, Mass., 1958), pp. 339-41 and *passim*.

16. On the Mennonites, see Benjamin Heinrich Unruh, *Die niederdeutschen Hintergründe der mennonitischen Ostwanderung im 16., 17. und 19. Jahrhundert* (Karlsruhe, 1955); A. H. Unruh, *Die Ges-*

chichte der Mennoniten-Brudergemeinde, 1860-1954 (Winnipeg, 1954). For Old Believers, Robert O. Crummey, *The Old Believers and the World of Anti-Christ: The Vyg Community and the Russian State, 1695-1855* (Madison, 1970), is especially informative.

17. de Kiewit, *op.cit.*, p. 76.

18. A famous work of Brazilian literature portrays this encounter, Enclides da Cunha, *Os Sertões*, translated by Samuel Putnam, ed., *Rebellion in the Backlands* (Chicago, 1944).

19. Why the United States did not abolish slavery peaceably whereas other slave-holding societies did so is an interesting question that deserves more investigation. For a recent and very persuasive analysis of why southern poor whites rallied to the slaveholders' interest as they did, see George M. Frederickson, *White Supremacy*, pp. 150-62.

20. Jerome Blum, *The End of the Old Order in Rural Europe* (Princeton, 1978), provides a magistral overview.

21. de Kiewit, *op.cit.*, pp. 88-276, gives a clear and coolly critical account of South African labor practices and race policy. Frederickson, *op.cit.*, pp. 199-238, illuminates differences between recent American and South African patterns of racial and industrial labor relations.

22. Hugh Tinker, *A New System of Slavery: The Export of Indian Labour Overseas, 1830-1920* (London, 1974), provides a detailed picture of how Indian coolie labor was recruited, exported, maltreated, and shipped back to India. Tinker's approach is descriptive and moral rather than statistical.

23. Statistics for Indian indentured labor come from Kingsley Davis, *The Population of India and Pakistan* (Princeton, 1951), pp. 99, 115-20. On indentured labor as a substitute for slavery see Stanley L. Engerman, "Servants to Slaves to Servants: Contract Labor and European Expansion," forthcoming in E. van den Boogaart and P. C. Emmer, eds., *Colonialism and Migration: Indentured Labour Before and After Slavery* (The Hague: Martinus Nijhoff/Leiden University Press, Comparative Studies in Overseas History, Vol. VI). I owe my understanding of the matter to this paper.

24. The figure of 46.2 million comes from Engerman, *op.cit.*, that for Russian colonization from Donald W. Treadgold, *The Great Siberian Migration* (Princeton, 1957), pp. 33-35.

25. The south, nevertheless, invented legal forms of labor contracts that preserved a good deal of compulsion for Blacks after 1863. See

William Cohen, "Negro Involuntary Servitude in the South, 1865-1940: A Preliminary Analysis," *Journal of Southern History* 42 (1976), 31-60.

26. Market exposure closely resembles disease exposure. Initial intrusion of civilized diseases upon a previously isolated community is always disastrous; similarly, market relations initially destroy local subsistence economies and traditional ways of life. Sporadic exposure remains costly too. For diseases, this means periodic epidemic with sudden, severe, and unpredictable die-off of young and old; for market relations it provokes the acute frictions between buyer and seller that characterized frontier life and upon which I have put considerable emphasis in these lectures. But, in both instances, fuller and more continuous contacts diminish costs. Endemic infection concentrates disease deaths among easily replaced infants even if lethality is not diminished, as usually also occurs; and full exposure to market options allows suitably conditioned individuals to profit from alternative opportunities by choosing shrewdly what do and with whom to make contracts. The economic equivalent of infant die-off also exists among those who, for whatever reason, remain incompetent in a market environment, making wrong choices and offering themselves as victims for more calculating and ruthless individuals. The history of civilization could, perhaps, be written around the way exchanges among human beings have altered through time in response to evolving patterns of transport and communication that always disseminated potent disease germs and no less potent goods and services, and did so in ever-changing ways.

27. Alfred Chandler, *The Visible Hand: The Managerial Revolution in America* (Cambridge, Mass., 1977), has instructive things to say about the development of corporate management since 1880.

28. Cf. the critique of Turner's ambivalence between the values of "civilization" and "cultural primitivism," in Henry Nash Smith, *Virgin Land: The American West as Symbol and Myth* (Cambridge, Mass., 1950), Ch. 22.

Index

Kaffirs 27, 40, 41

Latin America 5, 19, 35, 45, 46, 48

manufacture 28, 37
market allocation of re-
  sources 21-23, 48, 55-58, 70
Marxism 6, 7
Mennonites 43, 44
métis 42
Mexico 25, 34, 40, 48
Middle East 32
migration 18, 19, 22, 29, 37, 50, 51-54, 59
mining 19, 21, 42, 49, 54, 56
Mormons 42, 43, 68
Moslems 10, 17, 59

Napoleonic Wars 38
neolithic 12
New Zealand 18, 55, 56
North America 4, 5, 12, 13, 15, 17, 18, 19, 20, 27, 35, 39, 42

Old Believers 43, 44

Paulistas 41-42
peons, peonage 23, 25, 48
Peru 13, 34, 51
population growth 31, 32, 34, 35, 40
protection costs 11, 26, 27
Prussia 48
Puritans 42, 43

race mixture 34, 46
Rumania 14, 36, 45, 48

Russia 14, 15, 17, 18, 25, 26, 34, 43, 44, 48, 56-57

sectarian frontier communities 42-44
serfs, serfdom 20, 21, 23, 24, 45; abolition of 48
shipping 15, 18, 20-21
Siberia 15, 17, 24, 52, 53, 57
slaves, slavery 9, 19, 20, 21, 23, 24, 25, 34, 40, 41, 45, 48, 49,`51, 52; abolition of 47-48, 49, 55, 56
slave trade 17, 19, 47, 51
social hierarchy 20, 21, 22-23, 24, 25, 26, 27, 28, 31, 45, 48, 58, 60
Solomon Islands 48
South Africa 6, 12, 16, 18, 24, 39, 40, 41, 44, 49, 55
South America 4, 12, 17, 39. *See also* Latin America
Spain 15, 16, 19, 45
steppe nomads 11, 12, 14, 26

Tartars 26
trade 15, 17, 19-20, 23, 24, 27-28, 46-47, 55
trading companies 21, 28
transportation and communica-
  tion 11, 13, 15, 18, 24, 38, 40, 46, 53, 58
Turner, Frederick Jackson 3, 4, 5, 6, 9, 11, 16, 20, 25, 60

Ukraine 14, 26, 28, 34, 45
United States 3, 4, 6, 7, 8, 18, 25, 26, 27, 28, 42-43, 46, 47, 52, 54, 55, 56, 57, 58, 60-61;

War of Independence 45;
  Civil War 47
USSR, *see* Russia

Webb, Walter 4, 5, 6, 8, 9, 11,
  25, 60
westward movement 14

World War I 56, 59
World War II 5, 7, 56, 59

Young, Brigham 43

Zanzibar 47
Zulu war 40

Previous
CHARLES EDMONDSON HISTORICAL LECTURES
published by Baylor University Press
1977-1978
Paul K. Conkin, *American Christianity in Crisis*:
"Religious Rationalism—God without a Redeemer"
and "Darwinism—Nature without a Creator."
1979-1980
Walter LaFeber, *The Third Cold War*: "The
Kissinger Response" and "The Carter Response."
1980-1981
Martin E. Marty, *Religious Crises in Modern America*:
"The Modernist Attraction, 1880-1925," and
"The Fundamentalist Attraction, 1925-1980."

Library of Congress Cataloging in Publication Data
McNeill, William Hardy, 1917-
The great frontier.

(Fourth Charles Edmondson Historical Lectures)
Includes index.
1. Social History—Addresses, essays, lectures. 2. Frontier and
Pioneer Life—United States—Addresses, essays, lectures. 3.
Emigration and Immigration—History—Addresses, essays, lectures.
4. Social Classes—Addresses, essays, lectures. 5. Labor Supply—
Addresses, essays, lectures. 6. Equality—Addresses, essays, lectures.
I. Title. II. Series: Charles Edmondson Historical Lectures ; 4th.

HN13.M4   1983   973   83-42567

ISBN 0-691-04658-1